WHAT IF MOUNTAIN LIONS DISAPPEARED?

By Theresa Emminizer

Gareth Stevens
PUBLISHING

Please visit our website, www.garethstevens.com. For a free color catalog of all our high-quality books, call toll free 1-800-542-2595 or fax 1-877-542-2596.

Library of Congress Cataloging-in-Publication Data

Names: Emminizer, Theresa, author.
Title: What if mountain lions disappeared? / Theresa Emminizer.
Description: New York : Gareth Stevens, [2020] | Series: Life without animals
Identifiers: LCCN 2018059063| ISBN 9781538238141 (pbk.) | ISBN 9781538238165
  (library bound) | ISBN 9781538238158 (6 pack)
Subjects: LCSH: Puma–Conservation–Juvenile literature. | Wildlife
  conservation–Juvenile literature. | Animal ecology–Juvenile literature.
Classification: LCC QL737.C23 E56 2020 | DDC 333.95/416–dc23
LC record available at https://lccn.loc.gov/2018059063

Published in 2020 by
Gareth Stevens Publishing
111 East 14th Street, Suite 349
New York, NY 10003

Designer: Laura Bowen
Editor: Theresa Emminizer

Photo credits: Cover, p. 1 Rosalie Kreulen/Shutterstock.com; pp. 3–24 (series art) De-V/ Shutterstock.com; p. 5 Baranov E/Shutterstock.com; p. 7 Tier Und Naturfotografie J und C Sohns/Photographer's Choice RF/Getty Images; p. 9 Pinkcandy/Shutterstock.com; p. 11 James Michael Kruger/Photographer's Choice RF/Getty Images; p. 13 (vultures) Ondrej Prosicky/Shutterstock.com; p. 13 (coyote) Jukka Jantunen/Shutterstock.com; p. 13 (bobcat) Jack Bell Photography/Shutterstock.com; p. 15 (mountain lion) Charles Krebs/ Corbis Documentary/Getty Images; p. 15 (butterfly) Patrick Foto/Shutterstock.com; p. 17 Dennis W Donohue/Shutterstock.com; p. 19 jo Crebbin/Shutterstock.com; p. 21 iva/ Shutterstock.com.

Printed in the United States of America

CPSIA compliance information: Batch #CS19GS: For further information contact Gareth Stevens, New York, New York at 1-800-542-2595.

CONTENTS

Boldface words appear in the glossary.

Wonderful Wildcats

Mountain lions go by many names. You might hear them called cougars, pumas, catamounts, or panthers. Weighing up to 220 pounds (100 kg), mountain lions are the largest wildcats in North America. What would happen if these big, powerful animals disappeared?

Home on the Range

Mountain lions live throughout Canada, the United States, and Central and South America in many **habitats**, including deserts, forests, mountains, and wetlands. They keep to themselves, living within large **ranges**. An adult male's range can cover more than 100 square miles (259 sq km).

What Harms Mountain Lions?

Today, mountain lion habitats are shrinking. New roads and cities are breaking up their ranges. Less space leads to more **conflict** with people. Every year, more than 3,000 mountain lions are killed. They're overhunted and shot by farmers who fear they'll eat their herds.

NEXT 10 MILES

Why Are They Important?

Mountain lions are a keystone **species**. This means other animals in their **ecosystem** need them to **survive**. As top predators, mountain lions hunt deer, moose, elk, and rabbits. By eating these animals, mountain lions stop their numbers from becoming too big for the ecosystem to handle.

Mountain lions also affect other predators like bobcats and coyotes. They hunt the same animals as mountain lions. **Competing** against mountain lions changes where these animals live and hunt. Vultures, which feed on dead animals, are also affected by the presence of mountain lions.

bobcat

coyote

vultures

13

Without Mountain Lions

The health of the whole ecosystem hangs on the mountain lion's presence to keep it balanced. If mountain lions disappear, prey **populations** will grow out of control. Deer will overeat plants. Species that need plants to survive, such as butterflies, will disappear.

What Would Happen?

Without plant roots to hold it in place, soil will wash into streams, drying them. As the disappearing plants and shifting soil change the habitat, invasive, or non-native, species can move in. These species can push out native animals and take over.

Facing Danger

Although there are still thousands of mountain lions in the wild, their numbers are dropping. The Florida panther, a kind of mountain lion, has fewer than 160 members left. If action isn't taken soon, their disappearance could create many problems.

Florida panther

19

You Can Help!

The world needs mountain lions. What can you do to make sure they survive? Share what you know! Be a voice for wildlife. Keeping mountain lions safe means keeping all the plants and animals within their ecosystem safe, too.

GLOSSARY

compete: to try to get something that something else is also trying to get

conflict: a struggle or clash

ecosystem: all the living things in an area

habitat: the place or type of place where a plant or animal naturally lives and grows

population: the number of animals of the same kind that live in a place

range: the area where something lives

species: a group of plants or animals that are all of the same kind

survive: to live through something

FOR MORE INFORMATION

BOOKS

Rathburn, Betsy. *Mountain Lions.* Minneapolis, MN: Bellwether Media Inc., 2018.

Zuchora-Walske, Christine. *Mountain Lions.* Mankato, MN: Capstone Press, 2015.

WEBSITES

The Humane Society of the United States
humanesociety.org/animals/mountain-lions
Find out how you can help mountain lions.

National Geographic Kids
kids.nationalgeographic.com/animals/mountain-lion/
Learn more fun facts about mountain lions.

INDEX